How the

JET FIGHTER
F/A-18

McDonnell Douglas Hornet

by Frank Vann

Brian Trodd Publishing House

Contents

McDonnell Douglas F/A–18A Hornet

The McDonnell Douglas F/A–18A Hornet fighter aircraft has had a very mixed history. In fact, very few aircraft can have gone through so many changes of fate. Started by Northrop as what promised to be a new type of light-weight fighter, it was not accepted by the Unites States Air Force. Then it was modified, accepted as a winner, rejected again and finally transformed into a very successful carrier-based fighter in cooperation with a different manufacturer who produces it under his own name.

Today it is not just a fighter but also a very good ground attack aircraft. It can attack heavy tanks as well as ships. Its missiles can destroy reinforced concrete fortifications.

Even in its later form, it has been the subject of many modifications and has been fitted with weapons which were not considered when its design was started.

It all began in May 1966, when the Northrop company produced the design for a new fighter aircraft which was known as the P530. It was to carry air-to-surface weapons in addition to performing as a conventional fighter.

Basically, the function of fighter aircraft is to shoot down enemy aircraft which are trying to attack targets in the fighter's own country. They also have to act as escorts for their own attacking bombers and prevent enemy fighters from shooting them down. To do this they are armed with guns and air-to-air missiles.

The P530 was designed for this role in the first place but it was realised that by equipping it with air-to-surface missiles it could also act as an attack aircraft in an offensive role.

The aircraft was very compact and much smaller and lighter than other proposals of the same time. It weighed only 23,000 lb (10,440 kg). It had two General Electric engines and was given the name "Cobra".

The advantages of a small, light-weight fighter were seen to be that it would be cheaper to build and cheaper to maintain and

A Hornet of the Blue Angels display team taxis out for take-off.

operate. One big factor in its favour would also be that it would be more difficult for the enemy to pick it up on radar.

Unfortunately for Northrop, nobody at that time seemed interested in a small fighter and there was very little chance of getting an order from the United States Air Force.

In 1971, Northrop came up with the idea of building the Cobra with the help of foreign manufacturers whose governments might place an order for it. At that time, a number of the NATO countries could have been interested in joining Northrop in producing a new aircraft as a replacement for their ageing F–104 fighters.

This idea had hardly been launched when the Pentagon had a sudden change of mind and decided that there might be some use in buying a light-weight fighter after all.

So, Northrop polished up its design and put it forward in February 1972 in competition with proposals from four other companies. When the results were announced, the Northrop design came second. The aircraft chosen as the best was a design by General Dynamics.

Four Hornets of VFMA-451 "Warlords" armed with a mixture of bombs and air-to-air missiles.

The next surprise was that Northrop and General Dynamics were declared to be joint winners of the competition for the light-weight low-cost fighter to be known as the VFAX. Northrop set about building two prototypes of their aircraft which was given the code name YF–17.

The aircraft flew for the first time on 9 June 1974. It was so successful in its flight trials that even the important people who until then had been against light-weight fighters were beginning to change their minds. They decided that it was a good thing after all and started to support it.

By September 1974, the United States Air Force was saying that it wanted 650 of the aircraft and the future for Northrop was beginning to look very promising. Altogether, the F–17 appeared to have a bright future.

Meanwhile, General Dynamics had been carrying on with the design and manufacture of their aircraft which was known as the F-16.

The final blow fell on Northrop in January 1975 when the Air Force Secretary made it known that the winner of the light-weight fighter competition was not the Northrop design but the General Dynamics F–16.

The response of Northrop to this decision was courageous. The company resolved to carry on with what they knew was a good design. They realised that the F–16 was a better aircraft in some respects than the YF–17 but they still believed that, with some modifications, their design could turn into a very successful fighter aircraft.

At this stage, McDonnell Douglas appeared on the scene. McDonnell Douglas had realised that, with their expertise and experience in the design of fighter aircraft, the YF–17 could be developed to meet the requirement for a new carrier-based fighter for the United States Navy. After a lot of negotiations, it was agreed that Northrop

and McDonnell Douglas would work together to design and produce a new fighter. A new proposal was prepared and submitted in the spring of 1975.

The design bore a close resemblance to the "Cobra". The aircraft was to be a low cost light-weight fighter and was given the shortened name of NACF (Navy Air Combat Fighter). The aircraft was to operate from aircraft carriers and be capable of carrying out a number of attack missions as well as acting as a fighter.

McDonnell Douglas were to be the prime contractors with Northrop as the principal sub-contractor.

Two separate versions were considered at first. Both were to be single seater aircraft. The first was to be known as the F–18A and was to be a fighter. It would replace the F–4 Phantoms and be armed with Sparrow air-to-air missiles. The second was to be the A–18 version intended for attack missions.

In the end, the two versions came out so much alike that it was decided that one version would satisfy both requirements. It was to be known as the F/A–18A and has remained so ever since.

The design of a carrier-borne aircraft requires a great deal of skill from the engineers who have to produce the final plans.

In the first place, it is very much more difficult to take off and land on an aircraft carrier than on a fixed runway such as an airport. The sea is very rarely calm. As a result, the deck of the carrier is often moving in all directions at once. It heaves up and down. It rolls from side to side and it pitches backwards and forwards.

In rough sea conditions, the visibility is often very poor. The carrier deck is small compared to the size of an airfield on land. The sea does not present any landmarks which the pilot can use when finding his way

This series of plan-views shows the stages In the development of the F-18 Hornet from the P530 Cobra.

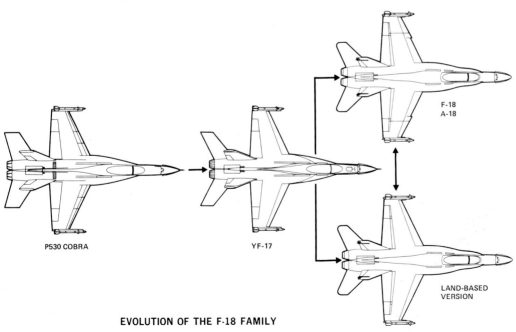

P530 COBRA

YF-17

F-18
A-18

LAND-BASED
VERSION

EVOLUTION OF THE F-18 FAMILY

back to the carrier. In any case, the carrier will not be where he left it when he took off.

When he is trying to land, none of this is of much help to the pilot who is trying to get all his wheels on to the deck at the same time. At the last moment before touchdown, he needs to adjust the motion of his aircraft to the motion of the carrier. His task is not made any easier by the fact that the carrier is probably sailing into the wind, so the air in which the aircraft is flying is moving fast relative to the deck.

The first feature that the aircraft needs is a wide-track undercarriage so that it will be stable and not tend to fall over sideways as the deck of the carrier rolls from side to side.

Secondly, because the deck of an aircraft carrier is very much shorter in length than the runway of a land airfield, the aircraft must be able to take off and land in a very short distance.

An F/A-18 Hornet comes in for a deck landing. Its under-carriage is down and the arresting wire further down the deck. The aircraft is armed with Sidewinder air-to-air missiles on its wing tips.

The steam catapult of the USS Coral Sea launches a Hornet which is carrying long-range fuel tanks under its wings. Another Hornet is already in position for launching.

The take-off can be shortened by launching the aircraft by means of a catapult, which is attached to the nose leg of the undercarriage. This means that the nose leg has to be very strong to carry the enormous loads needed to accelerate the aircraft along the deck for take-off. But it does ensure that the aircraft can get away with its full load of armaments and sufficient weight of fuel for a long mission.

The landing run is shortened by fitting a retractable arrestor hook below the fuselage of the aircraft. During landing, this hook is lowered on a long arm trailing underneath the rear fuselage. Stretched across the deck of the carrier are strong cables, each with shock absorbers at their outer ends. On landing, the pilot has to position the aircraft so that the hook catches in the cables and soon brings the aircraft to a stop.

The arrested landing also imposes very big stress loadings which have to be taken into account in the design of the structure of the aircraft.

Today, electronic systems can be used to assist the pilot in landing on aircraft carriers but it is still a manoeuvre which takes a lot of skill.

Finally, the environment on the deck of the carrier is not the ideal place for operating aircraft. The salt-laden atmosphere soon causes corrosion in the aluminium alloy structure if it is not properly protected. Special chemical treatments have to be applied to all the parts of the aircraft structure before they are assembled. This treatment makes them very resistant to salt spray.

A sea atmosphere is also not the ideal environment for the delicate electronic circuits which are to be found in all modern aircraft.

All of these difficulties can be overcome if allowance is made for them in the design of the aircraft and its systems. But they all add

This view is taken looking forward from underneath the rear fuselage of the Hornet. The striped bar in the centre is the arm carrying the arrestor hook which is the box-like unit nearest to the camera.

to the difficulty of producing an aircraft which is going to operate successfully for many years from aircraft carriers, often in emergency war conditions.

As we shall see, satisfactory solutions to all of these problems have been found in the case of the F/A–18A.

The work done by the aircraft designers of Northrop and McDonnell Douglas resulted in an aircraft which looks very much like the YF–17 but is, in fact, quite different.

The F/A–18 is a bigger aircraft than the YF–17. It weighs about twice as much. It is fitted with new engines which produce more power. Its undercarriage is redesigned for landing on carriers and strengthened to carry the loads involved in catapult launches and arrested landings.

The capacity of the fuel tanks has also been doubled, which results in a much improved range of operations.

In order to make it easier to store the aircraft in the hanger of an aircraft carrier, the wing now includes a wing-folding mechanism which reduces the wing span on the ground.

In May 1975, the new aircraft was named the "Hornet" and an initial order was placed by the United States Navy.

The first of the prototype aircraft flew on 18 November 1978 from the McDonnell Douglas airfield in St Louis.

After some initial problems with the rate of roll, the aircraft soon proved itself to be outstanding with extremely good handling behaviour. Because of this, it has been very popular with its pilots who regard it as being very easy to fly.

All modern aircraft are subjected to extensive strength testing to ensure that they will safely survive all the loads applied to them in service. In this picture we see a Hornet being dropped on to its undercarriage in a test which represents the conditions as the aircraft lands on the deck of an aircraft carrier.

The two drawings below show the Hornet in side view and head-on, and the same aircraft is shown in plan view opposite. This aircraft is shown equipped with Sidewinders at the wing tips and Sparrows at the wing roots. The head-on view below shows the wing folding, which saves valuable space in the hangar of an aircraft carrier. The side view shown opposite bottom right illustrates the two seat trainer version which has a larger cockpit canopy.

Dimensions

Wing span: 11.43 metres (37 ft 6 in)
Wing root chord: 4.04 metres (13 ft 3 in)
Wing tip chord: 1.68 metres (5 ft 6 in)
Aspect ratio: 3.5
Wing area: 37.16 sq metres (400 sq ft)
Sweepback at quarter chord: 20 degrees

Overall length: 17.07 metres (56 ft)
Height: 4.66 metres (15 ft 3½ in)
Width with wings folded: 8.38 metres (27 ft 6 in)

Weights

Empty weight: 10,455 kg (23,050 lb)
Take-off weight (fighter mission): 16,650 kg (36,710 lb)
Take-off weight (attack mission): 22,330 kg (49,220 lb)

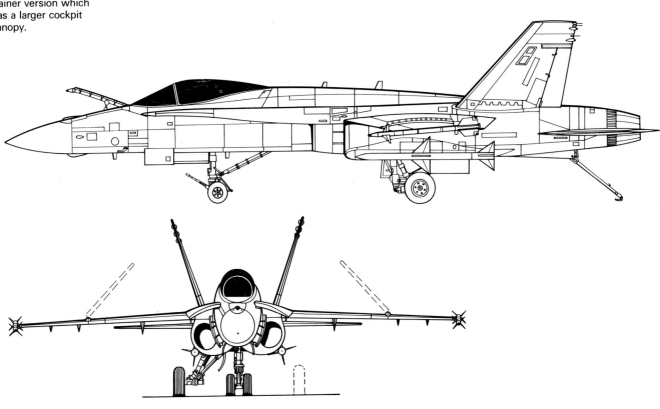

Performance

Combat ceiling: 50,000 ft
Maximum speed: Greater than M = 1.8
Radius of action (fighter mission): Over 740 km (460 miles)
Radius of action (attack mission): Over 1065 km (662 miles)
The aircraft can accelerate from 460 knots to 920 knots in less than two minutes at an altitude of 35,000 feet.

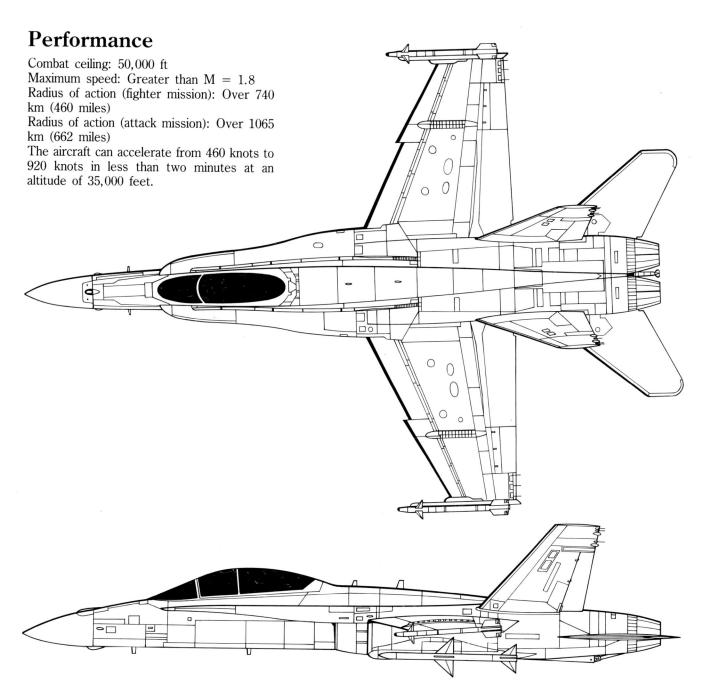

Distinguishing features

In the air the Hornet gives the impression of being a very busy little aircraft. Somehow its tail unit makes it look like an extremely aggressive insect.

As it only has to house one pilot, the fuselage is very slim. However, the wing root forward extensions fatten the part immediately in front of the wing leading edge. These extensions are one of the most successful design features of the aircraft. They help to guide the air into the engine intakes. In this way, they enable the aircraft to operate successfully at very high angles of attack – that is, with the nose pointing upwards very sharply.

The two engines are installed underneath the trailing edges of the wings. The air intakes are close in to the sides of the fuselage and the jets exhaust through twin jet pipes at the extreme end of the fuselage between the tailplanes, or "stabilators" as they are sometimes known.

The wings are only moderately swept back. They are straight tapered and end in square tips where missiles are usually installed. They have an anhedral of 3 degrees. In other words, instead of being horizontal or sloping upwards like the wings of most aircraft, they slope downwards when looked at from the front. This is clearly seen in the three-view general arrangement drawing of the aircraft.

The horizontal tail surfaces are behind the fins. They look like a normal tailplane but, in fact, they do more than the tailplanes and elevators of most other aircraft. They not only control the aircraft when the pilot wants to climb or dive, but also act as ailerons to control the rolling of the aircraft.

The most distinctive features of the aircraft are probably the fins. There are two of these which spring from the top side of the rear fuselage. They are not upright but lean outwards at about 20 degrees to the vertical.

A wide variety of missiles, fuel tanks or bombs can be carried externally at the wing tips, under the wings or hung from the bottom of the fuselage. Missiles can also be installed on the sides of the fuselage underneath the wings. All of these will be described in more detail later in this book.

This colourful picture shows a Hornet of the US Marine Corps carrying Sidewinders at the wing tips and Sparrows at the wing root stations.

The arrangement of the double fins on the top of the fuselage is clearly seen in this plan view. The arrestor hook can just be seen between the jet pipes.

Opposite above:
The leading and
trailing edge flaps are
moveable surfaces
which the pilot uses to
control the aircraft in
flight. When they are
deflected, they change
the curvature of the
wing section and
produce more lift. This
allows the pilot to land
and take off at much
lower speeds than he
could safely use
with the basic
wing section.

A closer look

The official description of the F/A–18A says
that it is a single-seat naval multi-mission
fighter. This means that it is basically a fighter aircraft designed to operate from aircraft
carriers. The "multi-mission" part presum-
ably means that it can also act in an attacking
role by carrying air-to-ground missiles and
bombs.

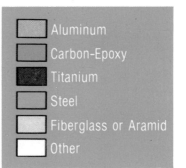

Aluminum
Carbon-Epoxy
Titanium
Steel
Fiberglass or Aramid
Other

A number of different
materials are used in
the construction of the
Hornet. Aluminium
high strength alloys
are the most widely
used but there is also
a large amount
of carbon-epoxy
composite material.
The colour coding in
the diagram indicates
the location of the
various materials used.

Wing

The wing is a cantilever structure with a number of internal beams or spars made of aluminium alloy. The skins are made of carbon fibre, partly as a means of increasing the stiffness of the wing box. Early flight trials showed that the aileron power was lower than required and the rate of roll was not as good as expected. The purpose of the ailerons is to increase the lift on one wing and reduce it on the other so that the aircraft rolls. On the early models, in addition to producing the lift to roll the aircraft, the ailerons were twisting the wing in a direction which opposed the roll. It was decided that the problem could be cured by increasing the torsional stiffness of the wing box so that it would not twist as much when the ailerons were used. This was done by using carbon fibre instead of aluminium alloy for the top and bottom skins. Carbon fibre composite material is much stronger and stiffer than metal even though it is also much lighter.

All along the leading edge of the wings there are flaps which assist the aircraft to manoeuvre. Along the trailing edge there are single-slotted flaps. When these are lowered they increase the lift on the wing during the landing and take-off phases when the speed is low. They are operated by hydraulic power.

To increase the power of the flaps, the ailerons also can be deflected symmetrically on both sides of the aircraft. This means that the flaps effectively cover the whole span of the wings and reduce the landing speed even further. Because of the short length of the deck of a carrier this is an important improvement. A lower landing speed also reduces the loads when the arrestor hook is used to stop the aircraft, because the energy to be absorbed is less when the aircraft is flying more slowly.

For Take-off/Landing

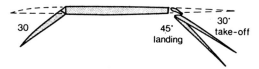

30   45° landing   30° take-off

For Manoeuvring

25°   variable for manoeuvring and cruise   20°

Below:
The pilot has a wide variety of control surfaces available to him for manoevering in flight. The horizontal stabilisers are used to make the aircraft dive or climb. The ailerons together with the rudders are used to bank the aircraft in a turn. The speedbrake produces drag when it is extended and slows the aircraft down. The use of the flaps is explained in the illustration above.

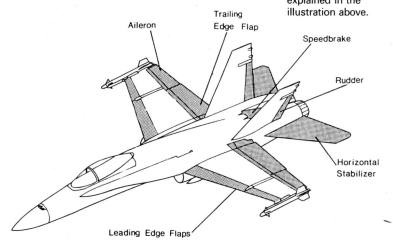

Aileron

Trailing Edge Flap

Speedbrake

Rudder

Horizontal Stabilizer

Leading Edge Flaps

The flap and aileron angles are decided by a computer in the aircraft. It works out which angles will give the most lift with the least drag in any particular set of circumstances. Lowering the flaps increases the lift but also increases the drag, so that the engine has more work to do in pushing the aircraft through the air. Because it is so important to use as little fuel as possible in a battle, it is very useful to have a computer which tells the pilot the most economical way to use the flaps or the ailerons.

Because the room available for the storage of the aircraft below the deck of a carrier is very limited, the wings have a hinge built in at the inner end of the ailerons. This enables the wings to fold upwards at about a right angle and thus reduce the span of the aircraft.

Fuselage

The structure of the fuselage is made mainly of high strength aluminium alloy with the usual arrangement of frames and skin panels. Some carbon fibre is used for access doors.

The engines are installed in the rear of the fuselage beneath the wing. Between the engines is a firewall made of titanium alloy. Titanium is used because it is very fire-resistant. If one engine catches fire, the fire is contained by the firewall until the extinguishers have put it out. The flames cannot reach the other engine and the aircraft can get home safely on one engine.

There is a dive-brake mounted in the top of the fuselage between the fins. This is pushed open by hydraulic jacks to create more drag when the pilot wants to slow down the aircraft as quickly as possible. The brake is made of carbon fibre.

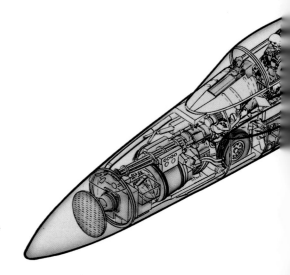

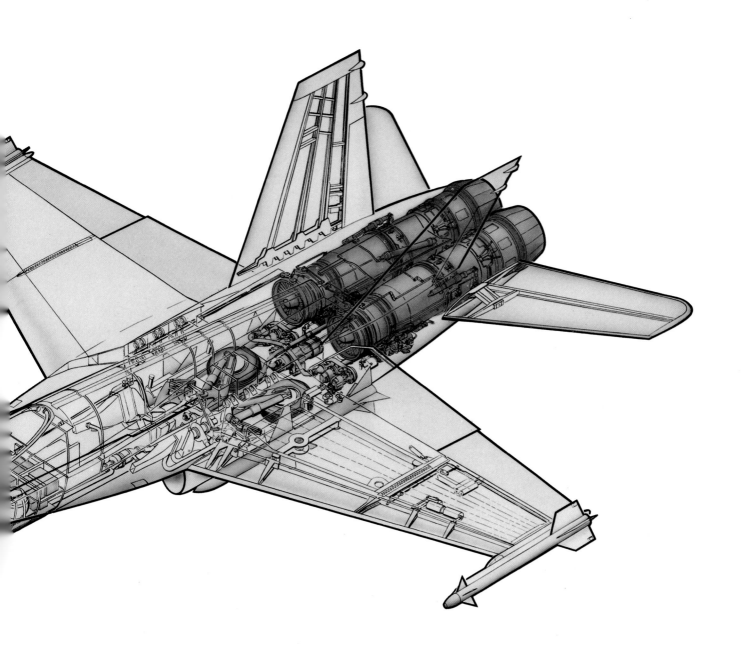

Tail surfaces

The fins and tailplane are made of carbon fibre composite materials. The way they are made is by using a carbon fibre composite sandwich with an aluminium alloy filling. The carbon fibre skins are supported by a honeycomb core made of thin aluminium alloy. Aluminium sheet is folded and glued so that it forms a block with a structure the same as that of the honeycomb in a beehive. The block is then machined to the shape of the aerofoil section and the carbon fibre skins glued on. The result is an extremely light and stiff structure which is very strong.

The moving parts of the tailplanes or stabilators are used to control the aircraft in pitch and in roll. If they are both moved downwards together they increase the lift load on the tailplane and the aircraft lifts its tail and

dives. Similarly, if they are both moved up together, they cause the aircraft to climb.

That is how the elevators act on a conventional aeroplane. However, on the F/A–18 they are given an additional job to do. They can be moved in opposite directions on the two sides. This has the effect of trying to lift one tailplane and lower the other. In this way they act like the ailerons in rolling the aircraft.

The rudders mounted on the fins are used to yaw the aircraft, that is to turn it from side to side. When they are nominally central they both point inwards. Because the fins are canted at an angle outwards from the vertical, this produces a down load which helps to pull down the tail of the aircraft.

All of the moveable control surfaces are operated by hydraulic jacks and are made of carbon fibre.

A close-up view from behind the aircraft shows the twin fins projecting from the outside of the engine bays.

Undercarriage

The undercarriage of the F/A–18 is very strong, so that it can stand up to the loads involved in operating from an aircraft carrier.

We have already mentioned some of the difficulties involved in landing an aircraft on the deck of a moving carrier. For instance, if the sea is very rough with big waves, the carrier might be heaving up and down under the action of a big wave as the aircraft is coming in to land. In this case, the landing deck may be rising rapidly at the moment when the aircraft is just about to touch down on it. This makes the impact between the wheels and the deck much heavier. That is why the undercarriage has to be designed for much bigger shock loads than a land-based aircraft.

The nose-leg has two wheels side by side. The inflation pressure of the tyres is 24 bars (350 lb/sq in) for operations from carriers but can be reduced for land-based operations. The wheels can be steered by the pilot to enable him to manoeuvre the aircraft on the ground.

In flight the nose-leg retracts forwards into the fuselage where it is covered by doors.

When the aircraft is catapult-launched from the carriers, the attachment for the catapult is on the nose-leg. A very large load is required to accelerate twenty tonnes of aircraft up to flying speeds within the length of a carrier deck. The nose-leg has to transmit that big load up into the fuselage, the wing and the engines so it has to be designed to be very strong.

The main undercarriages each have only one wheel. Like the nosewheel, the tyre pressure is 24 bars (350 lb/sq in). [The pressure in the tyre of a domestic car is only about 1.5 bars (24 lb/sq in)]. The legs retract backwards and are stowed in the bottom of the engine air intake ducts. The wheels have to turn through 90 degrees while they are being retracted so that they can fit into the space available.

Engines

The two engines are made by General Electric. They are GE F404 low bypass turbofans. In bypass engines, not all of the air passes through the hot core of the engine. Some of it is diverted by a fan to flow outside the engine and bypass the main flow. That is why they are called "bypass engines". Many modern civil aircraft engines have bypass ratios of 10 or more. That is, ten times as much air goes round outside the engine as goes through the hot working section and most of the thrust is produced by the fan.

In the case of the F404 engine the bypass ratio is only 0.34, so that almost all of the thrust comes directly from the jet efflux.

The engine can produce a thrust of 71.2 kN (16,000 lb).

As was said earlier, because of the clever design of the wing root extensions along the sides of the fuselage, the engines can keep running steadily when the intakes are pointing upwards or turned sideways at high angles to the flight path. This is obviously very useful in combat when the aircraft has to manoeuvre sharply to take evasive action. This important feature of the design was only obtained successfully after many flight trials and modifications.

In service the engine has proved extremely reliable. In fact, there have been almost no problems at all with the engines. The success of the aircraft is to a large extent because of their trouble-free behaviour.

When the aircraft is on the ground, it is necessary sometimes to have power available although the engines are not running. For this purpose the aircraft is fitted with an auxiliary power unit (APU) which is a miniature gas turbine made by Garrett and which provides electrical and hydraulic power. It also supplies the power for starting the main engines.

Fuel for the engines is carried in tanks in the wings and the fuselage. All of the tanks are self-sealing so that, if they are damaged by enemy fire, the holes will close up and no leaks will occur. This is obviously a most important point for aircraft which are going to be involved in air battles with enemy aircraft.

To extend the range of the aircraft, it can be refuelled from flying tanker aircraft. A flight refuelling probe is installed on the right-hand side of the fuselage in front of the cockpit. This can be extended in flight to engage the cone trailed by a tanker aircraft so that fuel is transferred into the tanks of the F/A–18.

The fuselage and wing tanks hold about 6,435 litres (1,415 gallons) of fuel. In addition, external tanks can be attached underneath the fuselage and at the inboard stations under the wings on each side. Each of these tanks can hold 1250 litres (275 gallons).

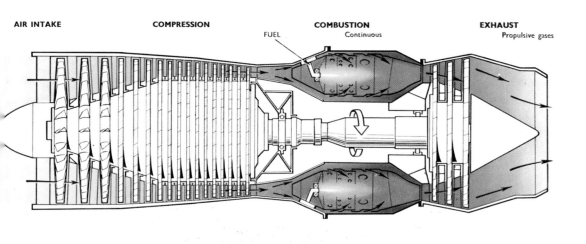

AIR INTAKE   COMPRESSION   COMBUSTION   EXHAUST

FUEL   Continuous   Propulsive gases

Jet engines produce thrust to propel the aircraft by sucking in air at the front intake and compressing it. Fuel is then injected into the compressed air and ignited. The heat of combustion causes the air to expand towards the rear end of the engine. The resulting jet of fast moving air produces thrust as it leaves the nozzle and propels the aircraft forwards. On its way to the exit nozzle the air also drives a turbine which is on the same shaft as the compressor at the front end of the engine. So more air is continuously forced into the engine and the cycle continues as long as there is fuel to keep it going.

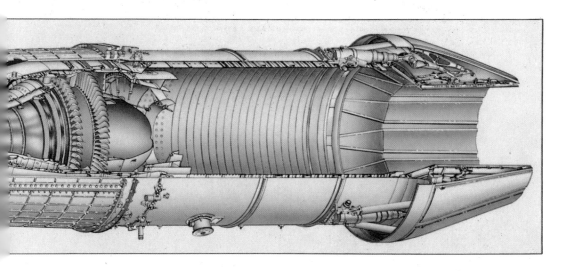

A cutaway view of the General electric F404 turbofan (its air intake is on the left and its exit nozzle is on the right). This engine has proved extremely reliable due mainly to the simplicity of its construction compared to its predecessors.

27

Systems

There is a fire detection system installed in the aircraft. This is equipped with heat sensors which immediately detect a fire and automatically operate an extinguishing system to put it out.

The pilot sits in a pressurised cockpit. There is so little air at the altitudes at which the aircraft will be operating that he would not be able to survive without the air which is pumped in to keep him alive. The outside air temperature is also very low, much lower than anywhere on the surface of the earth. Without heating, the pilot would freeze to death in a very short time. On the F/A–18, hot air is bled from the engines and circulated through the cockpit to keep the pilot warm.

When the cockpit is pressurised, it is in fact inflated like a balloon because the air pressure inside is bigger than that outside. If it were punctured by enemy fire in combat, therefore, it could burst like a balloon unless it were made strong enough. On the F/A–18, the fuselage obviously is strong enough and the cockpit structure is designed to be fail-safe. This means that if one of the structural members is cut by a bullet or a fragment of shrapnel, the other members near to it will

carry the loads and prevent the fuselage from failing.

The pilot sits in an ejector seat supplied by the British company, Martin-Baker, who specialise in the design of these seats. If the pilot has to get out of the aircraft in a hurry, he pulls a handle and he and his seat are fired upwards out of the aircraft by rockets built into the bottom of the seat. The canopy automatically gets out of the way to give him a free path out. His parachute then opens automatically. The Martin-Baker seat can even be used when the aircraft is standing on the ground. The ejector seat is projected so high above the aircraft that the parachute still has time to open fully and lower the pilot safely.

The pilot has in front of him one of the best displays of flight instruments in any fighter aircraft. The illustration shows the layout which faces him as he flies the aircraft.

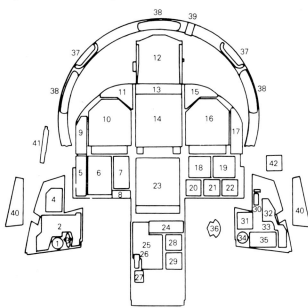

1. Brake pressure indicator
2. L/H vertical console control
3. Emergency/park brake
4. Landing-gear control
5. Stores jettison indicator
6. Digital engine monitor display
7. Fuel quantity indicator
8. Lightplate
9. Master arm panel
10. Master monitor display
11. Left threat display
12. Head-up display
13. HUD cameras
14. Up-front control panel
15. Right threat display
16. Multi-functional display
17. Map gain control
18. Attitude reference indicator
19. ECM display
20. Standby airspeed indicator
21. Standby altimeter
22. Vertical speed indicator
23. Horizontal situation display
24. Reserved for ECM
25. ECM control panel
26. Rudder pedal adjustment
27. Build-number plate
28. Clock
29. Pressurised compartmental altimeter
30. Arrestor hook
31. Height indicator
32. Landing lightplate
33. Wing-fold control
34. Hydraulic pressure indicator
35. Caution panel light
36. Static source selector
37. Canopy frame handle
38. Mirror
39. Shoot/lock indicator
40. Environmental control system louvre
41. Canopy jettison lever
42. Standby magnetic compass

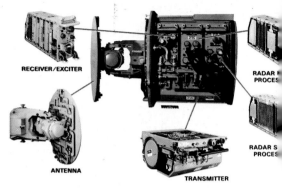

F/A-18 RADAR

RECEIVER/EXCITER

ANTENNA

TRANSMITTER

RADAR PROCES

RADAR S PROCES

Not only does the pilot have to manoeuvre the aircraft during combat. He also has to detect enemy targets and aim his weapons to attack them. He needs to monitor the performance of the engines. He has to navigate the aircraft to the target area and find his way back to the carrier, possibly in a wide expanse of ocean with no recognisable features.

In these tasks he is aided today by very clever electronic systems. However, even with these systems, the work load on the pilot becomes even more difficult because of the large amount of information being presented to him. The layout of the instruments and the way in which the necessary information is displayed become extremely important in determining the efficiency of the pilot. He must learn to look instinctively at the right place when he wants some vital information. A great deal of very serious thought, therefore, has to go into designing the arrangement of the flight instruments.

One way of lightening the burden on the pilot is to present the essential data in a head up display (HUD). This consists of a screen in front of the pilot through which he

has to look in order to fly the aircraft visually. Flight information can be projected on to this screen from below. As the pilot looks forward out of his cockpit, therefore, he sees not only the view ahead but also the instrument readings which he needs to pilot the aircraft. It looks as if the information were floating in the sky just ahead of him. By these means he can guide the aircraft by sight whilst, at the same time, reading all essential information from the flight instruments.

The head up display installed in the F/A–18 can be seen from the illustration showing the instrument layout.

When he is actually engaged in combat, it is necessary for the pilot to keep his hands on the control column and the throttle levers all the time. That is the only way in which he can manoeuvre the aircraft quickly enough to avoid being shot down himself. He cannot take his hands off the controls in order to fire his gun or launch a missile. This means that all the armament controls have to be built into the stick or the throttle levers so that he can operate them without letting go of the flight controls. This is known as

HOTAS (hands on throttle and stick) controls.

On the F/A–18 the pilot can fire the gun, launch air-to-air or air-to-ground missiles, operate his radar and disperse chaff to mislead enemy radars without taking his hand off the throttles or control column. It still requires a lot of practice to remember instinctively which button he should be pressing.

All modern aircraft are equipped with a range of electronic systems for navigation. In addition, combat aircraft have to carry systems for finding targets, for detecting hostile aircraft preparing to attack, for guiding missiles to home in on enemy installations and for warning the pilot if he himself is being detected by enemy radar.

The F/A–18 is fitted with an automatic carrier landing system (ACLS) which enables it to operate from aircraft carriers in any weather conditions. This helps the pilot to overcome some of the difficulties which were mentioned earlier but he still needs plenty of training before he can get his aeroplane down safely on the deck.

In wartime, the F/A–18 obviously has to perform an offensive role. It has to find enemy targets which may be hostile aircraft, ships, tanks or other military installations.

For this purpose, the aircraft is equipped with radar which enables it to track up to 10 different targets at the same time and inform the pilot of their positions.

Electronic counter-measures (ECM) play a large part in modern combat conditions. These are devices which disturb the enemy radar so that hostile forces are getting false information from their radar systems.

The F/A–18 has an airborne self protection jammer (ASPJ) and a system which warns the pilot if he has been picked up by enemy radar.

In 1979 this modified T-39A Sabreliner was fitted with the nose and radar of the Hornet (then in its preproduction stage) to test its radar and avionics systems.

31

The Hornet's Radar is the APG-65 which has several functions. It can map the terrain over which the aircraft is flying in rough detail, and map the central part of the field of vision very accurately (top left). Consequently the pilot always knows his precise location. In air combat the pilot can send a beam of pulses at the enemy plane (top centre). The APG-65 notes how long the pulses take to be reflected and sets the guns to fire in front of the enemy by the appropriate amount. When flying at low level (above right) the radar system enables the pilot to avoid mountains and other hazards. By using all the radar's facilities, the pilot can fly an indirect course to his unseen target and attack it on his first attempt (below).

The aircraft also has an inertial navigation system. This uses gyroscopes to determine the true path of the aircraft through the air in all three dimensions and it does not depend on any information obtained from outside the aircraft. Therefore, it cannot be interfered with by any outside agency.

The gyroscopes are made to extremely precise dimensions. As a result they are unbelievably accurate. They continually measure the acceleration of the aircraft in all three axes, vertically, sideways and in the forward direction. If the variation of the aircraft acceleration with time is known very precisely, it is possible to calculate its speed at any given time. In the same way, when the variation of speed with time is known, it is possible to calculate the distance travelled relative to the starting point.

All the time that the aircraft is in the air, an on-board system is monitoring and recording the performance of the aircraft, its engines and its systems. When the aircraft lands, this information shows where maintenance work is needed without the need for lengthy inspections.

Because of the risk of damage to the aircraft in battle conditions, there is a possibility that its controls might be put out of action by enemy fire. If it had only one system this would lead to the loss of the aircraft. To prevent this happening, the normal flight control system of the F/A–18 is a quadruply redundant system. This means that there are four independent flight control systems. If one is destroyed, there are still three left for the pilot to use. In fact, the aircraft can survive the loss of three systems and get home on the remaining one.

On the right-hand side of the instrument panel is a stand-by set of instruments giving airspeed, vertical rate of descent and altitude so that, if all else fails, the pilot can land the aircraft manually.

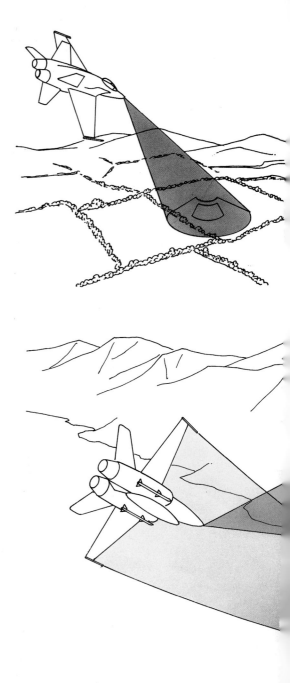

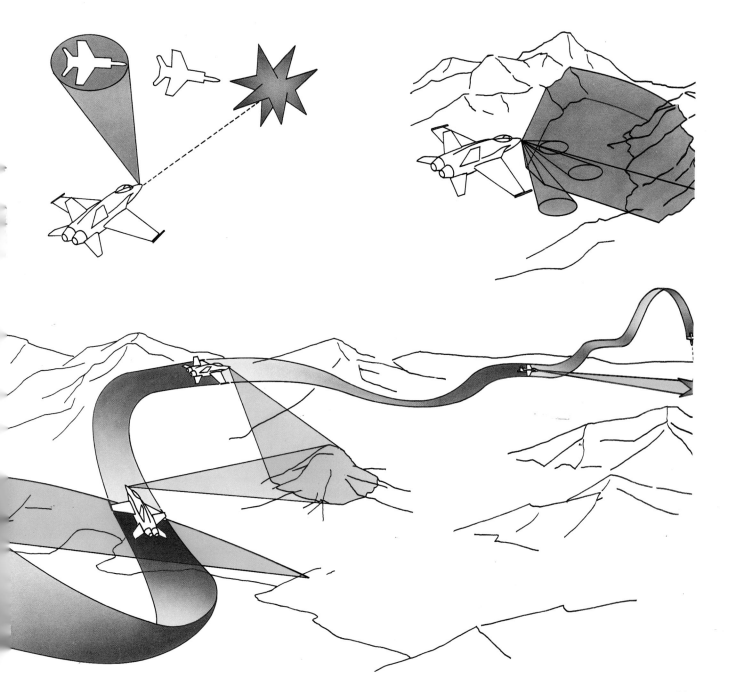

Although a small aircraft, the Hornet can carry a surprising load of armaments. Its total payload of 8170 kg (18,000lb) can include air-to-air and air-to-ground missiles, bombs and anti-submarine weapons. Right at the front of the display shown in the photograph is the 20mm gun with its ammunition spread out before it.

Armaments

The aircraft is armed with an M61 six-barrelled 20 mm gun installed in the nose of the fuselage. The magazine holds 570 rounds of ammunition, which can be fired in less than ten seconds. The aircraft is aimed by a McDonnell Douglas director gun sight backed up by a conventional gun sight.

Externally, there are nine weapon stations with a total carrying capacity of 7,710 kg (17,000 lb).

For reference, these are numbered 1 to 9 counting across from the left-hand wing tip. Station 5 is located under the centre of the fuselage. Stations 4 and 6 are on the sides of the fuselage and the other six stations are for weapons slung from the wings. The two wing tip stations (1 on the port wing and 9 on the starboard wing) usually carry AIM–9 Sidewinder air-to-air missiles.

The Sidewinder has been developed for over 30 years during which time it has continually been improved. It was first fired in trials in September 1953. Since then its homing devices have been made more effective. Later versions also have smokeless motors so that enemy pilots will find it more difficult to take evasive action to escape them.

The Sidewinder carries a high explosive warhead which fragments when it is detonated. It then fires out hundreds of metal fragments travelling at a very high speed which would disable, at least, any enemy aircraft near to it. It is guided to its target by an infrared homing system.

It is powered by a solid propellent rocket motor which is ignited as the missile leaves the launching rack.

The missile weighs 86 kg (190 lb) and is now manufactured in Europe as well as in the United States of America.

The F/A–18 can also carry AIM–7 Sparrow missiles. These are mounted at stations

Harpoon air-to-air missiles and anti-ship missiles are installed on this Hornet at the mid-wing stations. Also visible are the Sidewinder missiles at the wing tips.

2 and 8 under the outer wing or on the fuselage sides at stations 4 and 6.

The Sparrow is a medium range guided weapon which can be used in all weather conditions. It can find its way to the target through rain or fog. It is exploded by a contact fuse if it hits the target or by a proximity fuse if it passes close to it. The warhead contains 40 kg (88 lb) of high explosive so its effect is lethal.

The homing system is very effective and cannot easily be interfered with by electronic counter-measures.

The total weight of the missiles is 228 kg (503 lb). It is 3.6 metres (11 ft 10 in) long and has a wing span of 1 metre (3 ft 3 in). Like the Sidewinder, it has a solid propel-

lent rocket motor.

Later versions of the F/A–18 will carry the AIM–120A medium range air-to-air missile. At present this has no other name and is usually referred to as the AMRAAM missile.

The AMRAAM has been developed from an American design for use on European aircraft such as the Tornado. It is intended to replace the Sparrow in the near future.

It is a radar-guided missile capable of operating in all weather conditions. It can be launched against hostile aircraft before they are near enough to be seen. It is possible to launch 8 AMRAAMs simultaneously so that the Hornet will, in theory at least, be able to engage a whole squadron of enemy aircraft when it is equipped with the new missiles.

The Hornet launches a Sparrow air-to-air missile. The missile drops clear of the aircraft before the rocket motor ignites. The shock waves in the rocket exhaust are clearly visible.

The homing system of AMRAAM is much more ingenious than that of Sparrow or Sidewinder. The missile has an inertial guidance system to guide it most of the way to the place at which the F/A–18's radar has detected enemy aircraft. The missile needs to know where it is relative to the target at the moment when it is launched. This information is given to the computer in the missile at the moment it leaves the aircraft.

After it has been launched, the missile accelerates to supersonic speeds.

When the missile gets close to the target, its own radar system then starts to guide it on a closing course to the enemy until the fuse explodes the warhead.

Despite its extra capabilities, the AMRAAM weighs less than Sparrow. It turns the scales at 152 kg (335 lb).

It is 3.65 metres (12 ft) long and only 178 mm (7 in) in diameter.

All of the missiles described above are air-to-air weapons intended to shoot down enemy aircraft.

The Hornet can also carry a powerful selection of air-to-ground missiles. These can be used to attack targets such as tanks, ships, fortifications and ground installations.

Included among the weapons which can be carried by the F/A–18 are Maverick and Harpoon.

The AGM–65 Maverick is an air-to-surface missile produced by Hughes. It can be used effectively against hard targets such as armoured vehicles and concrete shelters.

It is guided by television or laser or infrared. If television is used the pilot of the F/A–18 can see a picture of the target on a

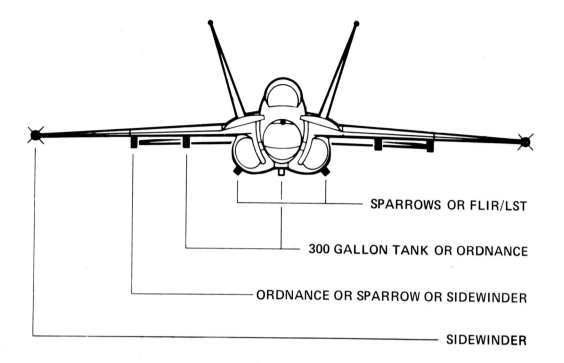

External stores or weapons can be carried at nine stations under the wing and fuselage of the Hornet.

SPARROWS OR FLIR/LST

300 GALLON TANK OR ORDNANCE

ORDNANCE OR SPARROW OR SIDEWINDER

SIDEWINDER

The AGM–84 Harpoon is an air-to-surface missile for use against shipping. It can be used to sink large vessels such as destroyers or freighters. It is also capable of dealing effectively with submarines if it is lucky enough to catch one on the surface.

The Harpoon is another product of McDonnell Douglas. An on-board computer screen in the cockpit and can guide the missile directly on to its destination.

The warhead is a 57-kg (125-lb) shaped charge which directs all the blast forward. It can punch a hole through thick armour plate or reinforced concrete.

Its range is anything from 0.9 to 24.2 km (0.5 to 15 miles).

Its total weight is about 225 kg (500 lb).

Mavericks are usually carried under the wings at the inboard stations 2, 3, 7 or 8.

calculates the flight path and guides the missile on its course until its radar picks up the target and homes in on it.

In the summer of 1986, an F/A–18A launched a Harpoon missile successfully for the first time. It is now intended to include the ability to use Harpoon in all aircraft.

Like Maverick, Harpoon is carried under the wings of the F/A–18 at stations 2, 3, 7 and 8.

Harpoon is a large weapon. It is 3.84 metres (12 ft 7 in) long and weighs 522 kg (1150 lb).

In addition to missiles, the Hornet can also carry bombs at any of the stations apart from the wing tips.

Rocket packs can also be fitted, as can a range of cameras and other equipment for reconnaissance purposes.

Variants

A number of different versions of the Hornet have already been announced and, no doubt, others have yet to appear.

Briefly, the versions in existence at the moment are:

F/A–18A
This was the original single-seat fighter equipped with Sparrow air-to-air missiles.

F/A–18B
A two-seater version used for training. The pilot and pupil sat one behind the other, which necessitated modifications to the fuselage.

F/A–18C and F/A–18D
These are improved versions of the F/A–18A and F/A–18B respectively.

They are equipped to carry more up-to-date weapons such as AMRAAM and Maverick. Their avionic systems are redesigned to new levels of effectiveness so that they are easier to operate and to maintain. They are also being developed for use at night in an attacking role.

Opposite above:
This view taken from above an unmarked Hornet emphasises its sharply swept back wings and tailplanes.

Opposite below:
The aircraft's high degree of manoeuvrability is seen to perfection in this example of close formation flying.

The fuselage of an F/A-18A of the Australian Air Force being carried on a transporter to the final assembly line.

F/A–18(R)
This version is to be used for reconnaissance. The gun is removed from the fuselage to make room for electronic equipment or cameras.

Australian F/A–18A/B

The Australian Air Force has ordered 57 single-seaters and 18 two-seaters in this version. Apart from the first two which were built in the United States, the aircraft were being assembled in Australia.

CF–18A and CF–18B
This is a version of the aircraft which has

been sold to the Canadian Air Force. The CF–18B is a two-seat version like the F/A–18B, to be used for training.

EF–18

The Spanish Air Force has bought 72 of these aircraft and has options for 12 more. Some of the manufacture is being done in Spain. CASA, the Spanish aircraft manufacturer in Madrid, is making a wide variety of components for the F/A–18 including the tail-planes, flaps, air brakes and rudders, most of which are made of carbon fibre composite material.

RF–18D

The United States Marine Corps, who also operate the British designed Harrier, will be taking delivery of this version at the end of 1990. It is intended for all-weather reconnaissance and is equipped with extremely sensitive radar in a pod mounted under the fuselage at station 5.

The aircraft, which are intended to operate from bases on the mainland, do not have the wing folding mechanism of the carrier-based aircraft.

Altogether it is intended to build 1157 Hornets of various versions. 150 of these will be the two-seater trainer version.

All of the essential controls must be located at the pilot's finger tips. The throttle and control stick are shown together with the switches and press-buttons needed to operate the radar, launch missiles and fire the gun.

A VFA-125 "Rough Riders" Hornet is loaded with armaments. This particular model was intended to be flown from aircraft carriers and underwent trials on the USS *Constitution* in 1982 but was found to be unsuitable for service at sea.

A Hornet is refuelled in flight via a drogue from the fuel tanker.

A US Marine Corps Hornet is refuelled from a U.S. Navy KA-3 tanker during a test flight.

The F/A–18 in Action

The Hornet saw active service for the first time in April 1986 when aircraft from the carrier *Coral Sea* took part in the raids on Libya.

The squadrons involved operate under the names of the "Wildcats", the "Privateers", the "Black Knights" and the "Death Rattlers".

Other exciting names used by F/A–18 squadrons are "Fist of the Fleet", "Rough Raiders", "Golden Dragons", "Warlords", "Thunderbolts" and "Gray Ghosts", to name but a few.

In Conclusion

This brings us up-to-date in the story of the McDonnell Douglas F/A–18 Hornet.

We began with the Northrop light-weight fighter project which has gone through many changes and improvements before turning into the very successful Hornet. McDonnell Douglas saw the possibilities waiting to be developed in the first design. Using their wide experience in the design of military aircraft, they have refined the initial concept into what could fairly be claimed to be the most successful fighter aircraft in service today.

Currently, the F/A–18s have completed over 300,000 hours of flying and it looks as if they will complete many hundreds of thousands more before they are withdrawn from service into an honourable retirement.

Four Hornets take part in a bombing exercise in Nevada. They are carrying MK-82 bombs and centreline fuel tanks.

Although this US Navy Hornet is flying into the sunset, this outstanding aircraft will remain in service into the next century.